Travel On and On

Interdisciplinary Lessons on the Music of World Cultures

ELISA MACEDO DEKANEY AND DEBORAH ALANE CUNNINGHAM

Published in partnership with
MENC: The National Association for Music Education

ROWMAN & LITTLEFIELD EDUCATION
A division of
ROWMAN & LITTLEFIELD PUBLISHERS, INC.
Lanham • New York • Toronto • Plymouth, UK

Published in partnership with MENC: The National Association for Music Education

Published by Rowman & Littlefield Education
A division of Rowman & Littlefield Publishers, Inc.
A wholly owned subsidiary of The Rowman & Littlefield Publishing Group, Inc.
4501 Forbes Boulevard, Suite 200, Lanham, Maryland 20706
http://www.rowmaneducation.com

Estover Road, Plymouth PL6 7PY, United Kingdom

British Library Cataloguing in Publication Information Available

Library of Congress Cataloging-in-Publication Data

Dekaney, Elisa Macedo, 1966–
  Travel on and on : interdisciplinary lessons on the music of world cultures / Elisa Macedo Dekaney and Deborah Alane Cunningham.
    p. cm.
  Includes bibliographical references.
  ISBN 978-1-60709-310-7 (cloth : alk. paper) — ISBN 978-1-60709-311-4 (pbk. : alk. paper) — ISBN 978-1-60709-312-1 (electronic)
  1. School music—Instruction and study—Social aspects. 2. Music—Cross-cultural studies. 3. Interdisciplinary approach in education.
I. Cunningham, Deborah Alane, 1968– II. Title.
  MT1.D453 2011
  780.71—dc22   2010028840

♾™ The paper used in this publication meets the minimum requirements of American National Standard for Information Sciences—Permanence of Paper for Printed Library Materials, ANSI/NISO Z39.48-1992. Printed in the United States of America

Contents

Introduction

Traditionally, music education certification programs across the United States have focused on preparing their students to teach the musical skills addressed by standards 1–7 of the National Standards for Music Education (Consortium of National Arts Education Associations, 1994). It is understood that every music teacher should be prepared to teach vocal and instrumental performance, music literacy skills, and improvisation and composition techniques, as well as strategies for listening to, describing, and evaluating music. Of equal importance, yet often overlooked, are Standard 8 (understanding relationships between music, the other arts, and disciplines outside the arts) and Standard 9 (understanding music in relation to history and culture). The main purpose of this book, *Travel On and On: Interdisciplinary Lessons on the Music of World Cultures*, is to inspire music educators to implement National Standards for Music Education 8 and 9 when teaching the varied music repertoire from our global cultures.

Inspired by the work of Barrett, McCoy, and Veblen (1997) in *Sound Ways of Knowing: Music in the Interdisciplinary Curriculum*, we began to explore ways through which the music from our world cultures could be taught in a more holistic and contextualized manner. *Travel On and On* features folk and newly composed musical materials suitable for the general music classroom, with connections to science, English language arts, dance, social studies, and languages other than English. As insightfully stated by Wiggins (2001):

> Integration through enhancement and thematic association are routinely practiced by many good teachers. However, it is teaching through conceptual and process connections that can provide opportunities for students to experience the world through a variety of perspectives, strengthening their capacity for cognitive development and enhancing the quality of their lives. This more holistic vision of integration is rooted in the belief and understanding that individuals have many ways of perceiving the world, that one way of thinking is not necessarily better than another, that who we are is determined by our ability to understand the world from a variety of perspectives, and that thinking and understanding transcend subject area distinctions. (p. 276)

Over the past thirty years, music educators in the United States have made significant efforts toward curricular changes in order to incorporate and effectively teach the music from our global community. It is essential, though, that the teaching of global music be accompanied by its social, geographical, and historical contexts. Therefore, over the past several years we have developed classroom lessons that feature music from various parts of the world and have direct connections to other subject areas. These lessons can be taught by music educators in collaboration with other content-area teachers, used by teachers of various subject areas with the support and musical expertise of music educators, or taught solely by the music teacher in his or her general music classroom. All the lessons included in this book have been taught at the middle school level, and have been presented in workshops for novice and expert music teachers in the United States.

The lessons in this book were designed as small unit plans rather than single lessons and should be taught over the course of several weeks. They are all based on the National Standards for the various subject areas and specifically conceived for the general music classroom. Each lesson, however, can be easily adapted for both choral and instrumental settings. The lessons focus on music from Latin America, Africa, and the United States with special emphasis on Native American, African American, and Cajun cultures. The lessons feature traditional folk music from various parts of the world as well as newly composed materials inspired by these specific world cultures. The majority of the lessons also incorporate the Orff-Schulwerk approach to music education.

Several sources from the World Wide Web have been suggested as tools to enhance student learning and teacher preparation. There are websites that provide free and reliable maps, videos, classroom activities, and other resources that support and assist in teaching the music of our global cultures. Music teachers are encouraged to take advantage of this body of information.

This book is divided into three chapters. The first chapter explores the connections between music and language arts. All lessons are accompanied by significant literature on the topic and provide an exciting opportunity for collaboration with the English language arts teacher. The final product of these lessons can also lead to a public performance in a concert setting, or simply for other classes and teachers. The first lesson, "Brazilian Music and Game: 'Os Escravos de Jó,'" introduces a Brazilian folk song that is accompanied by a table game and is extremely popular among children of all ages. It is designed to encourage students to create a dance choreography and ostinati that would accompany the folk song. The lesson also focuses on capoeira, the Brazilian martial arts, and its social and musical meaning. The second lesson, "Rhythms and Proverbs: Windows to the Cultures of Africa and Latin America," is a journey exploring the words of wisdom from countries in Africa and Latin America, accompanied by a newly composed song based in the Orff-Schulwerk tradition. As a result, all the parts of this lesson can be performed as part of a concert experience. The third lesson, "Fantastic Fables: Exploring Native American Culture," exposes students to the rich tradition of Native American fables and their meaning.

The second chapter presents connections between music and science. The first lesson, "The Life of a Snowflake: Exploring Hexachords, Hexagons, and the Water Cycle," encourages students to understand the uniqueness of each snowflake in terms of science and transfer that concept to the exceptionality of each individual. The second lesson, "Butterflies," begins with a light and fun science approach to understanding the beauty of the South American lepidoptera and how they are portrayed in a folk song. The lesson takes a radical turn when it examines children's poems written during World War II by interns of the Terezín ghetto in Czechoslovakia, and how contemporary composers have set some of these poems to music. The beauty, freedom, and colorful characteristics of the butterflies are terribly missed by these young children and poignantly portrayed in their poems.

The third chapter focuses on music from the United States influenced by French and African cultures. The first lesson, "Cajun Capers: Introduction to Cajun Culture," celebrates the Cajun culture and its significant contribution to American society through language, cuisine, dance, and music. The second lesson, "Slavery in the New World: Brazil and the United States," compares and contrasts the lives of Africans who were brought to the United States and to Brazil by exploring the inventive ways through which they fled captivity following the Underground Railroad path or finding shelter in the *quilombos*. The lesson also introduces the musical contributions of Afro-Brazilians. The third lesson, "Celebrating Spirituals," presents the great African American legacy of spirituals leading to the music performance of "Follow the Drinking Gourd" and "Wade in the Water" accompanied by Orff instruments.

These lessons are only a starting point of the endless journey of discovering the music of our global cultures through an interdisciplinary approach. The lessons were not conceived as final works; instead, they were created as organic cells that are always under transformation and adaptation. Our hope is that teachers will look into their own school communities and find inspiration for many more collaborations and lesson planning, always considering the best ways to reach our students and to teach them about our growing global community.

1

Music, Dance, and English Language Arts

BRAZILIAN MUSIC AND GAME: "OS ESCRAVOS DE JÓ"

National Standards

Music

Standard 1: Singing, alone and with others, a varied repertoire of music

Standard 2: Performing on instruments, alone and with others, a varied repertoire of music

Standard 3: Improvising melodies, variations, and accompaniments

Standard 8: Understanding relationships between music, the other arts, and disciplines outside the arts

Standard 9: Understanding music in relation to history and culture

In collaboration with the social studies teacher or alone, the music teacher may also address social studies standards, for example, New York State Social Studies Standards 2 and 3. These are available from www.emsc.nysed.gov/ciai/standards.html.

It is also possible to address National Standards for Dance Education 1 and 3, found in *National Standards for Arts Education* (Consortium of National Arts Education Associations, 1994).

Objectives

Students will learn to sing the melody of a song, "Os Escravos de Jó," in Portuguese.

Students will learn the movements to the passing game of the same name that accompanies the song, accurately transferring the visual spatial pattern in the game to their own hand movements.

Students will demonstrate accurate memorization and reproduction of the movement sequences of the passing game.

Students will compose short rhythmic ostinati to accompany the song.

Students will learn about traditional Brazilian instruments and play the rhythmic ostinati on similar percussion instruments.

Students will learn about capoeira, a Brazilian dance/martial arts, and will accurately describe it in writing.

Materials

Surdo drums (from Brazil) or drums of at least three sizes (low, medium, and high)

Paper or plastic cups or any other objects that students can use to play the game *Os Escravos de Jó*

Internet access (optional) to show capoeira movements on YouTube or other websites

Whiteboard

Process

Part I

1. Teacher introduces the song "O Escravos de Jó" (figure 1.1). It is a Brazilian folk song that accompanies a table game usually played at social dinners, parties, weddings, and other gatherings. Secular in nature, the lyrics sometimes are playful and humorous. *Os Escravos de Jó* (caxangá) is one of the most well-known table games in the states of São Paulo and Minas Gerais.

2. Teacher explains the game. In this game, each player takes a kitchen utensil, a cup, or a matchbox and passes it on to the person on the right, emphasizing the strong beat while singing the song. The objects are passed from hand to hand until the "zigue zigue zag" point in the song, where the player marks each beat with the object in hand in a lateral back-and-forth (right-left-right) movement (without releasing the object). The first time the player keeps the object, but the second time the player releases it and the song starts all over again. The purpose of the game is to increase the tempo until people who break the rhythm are eliminated and only one player is left. The person who remains until the end is the winner. This game is played by children and adults alike.

Portuguese: *O escravos de Jó jogavam caxangá*

IPA: *[os es'kɾavos ʤi ʒɔ ʒo'gavãw kaʃã'ga]*

Translation: *The slaves of Job played caxangá*

FIGURE 1.1. "Os Escravos de Jó"

Portuguese:	Tira, bota, deixa o Zé Pereira ficar
IPA:	[ˈtʃiɾa ˈbɔta ˈdejʃa o zɛ peˈɾejɾa fiˈkaɾ]
Translation:	Take it out, put it back, let Zé Pereira stay
Portuguese:	Guerreiros com guerreiros fazem zigue, zigue, zague
IPA:	[geˈxejɾos kõ geˈxejɾos ˈfazẽj ˈzigi ˈzigi zag]
Translation:	Warriors with warriors do zigue, zigue, zag

3. Students perform the song several times until the movement sequence is memorized and well coordinated.

4. Teacher divides the students into two or three groups and asks each group to compose a two-measure rhythmic ostinato in a binary beat (2/4). It is important that the second beat be the stronger one as opposed to the first. After composing the ostinato, students share it with the class using any kind of body movement (hands, legs, head, and so on).

5. Teacher writes all the ostinato patterns on the board.

6. Teacher introduces the Brazilian *surdo* drum (or equivalent) to the students. The *surdo* (Portuguese word for "deaf") is a double-headed cylindrical drum similar to the bass drum (figure 1.2). It is widely used in Brazilian music, especially for the samba. The rhythm of the samba usually requires three different sizes of *surdos*: a big drum playing on beat 2 called *resposta* (Portuguese word for "answer"), a medium drum playing on beat 1 called *marcador* (roughly translated as "the one who marks the beat"), and a smaller drum called *cortador* (Portuguese word for "cutter") playing also on beat 2 but adding a few more notes than the *resposta*. *Surdo* players use mallets when playing their instruments.

7. Teacher asks students from each group to choose a Brazilian (or similar) percussion instrument in which their ostinato pattern would sound the best. This group will teach the ostinato to everyone in the class. Teacher then divides the class into two groups, and one group sings the melody while the other plays the ostinato pattern. All groups should have the opportunity to share their ostinati.

8. Students perform "Os Escravos de Jó" with ostinato patterns that they just composed. Teacher encourages all students to alternate between singing the melody and playing all the ostinati.

9. After students have learned the music and the game it would be appropriate to have a small percussion accompaniment while part of the class plays the game. It is important to give everyone a chance to play the game, sing, and also play the instruments.

Part II

1. Teacher encourages students to create dance movements that would best choreograph, in their minds, the song "Os Escravos de Jó." Students should be able to freely move in the classroom and to express their dance ideas using the whole body to represent their musical feeling.

2. Teacher helps the students to work on a collective choreography, deciding which movements from each person best represent the ideas of the whole group.

3. Students perform the newly choreographed Brazilian folk song. The percussion instruments from the previous part can also be added to the performance.

4. Teacher introduces the capoeira, an Afro-Brazilian type of dance/martial arts (figure 1.3).

   Although the origin of capoeira is still uncertain, it is possible that it was brought to Brazil by the Africans from Angola. It was a way for the slaves to be physically fit in case they had the opportunity to escape or had to defend

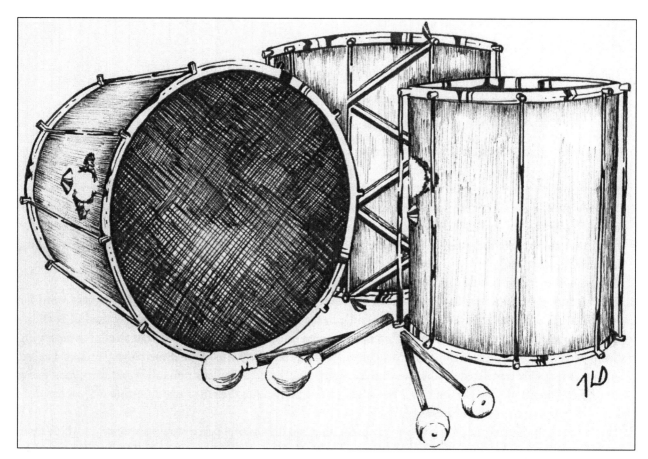

FIGURE 1.2.   Pen and Ink *Surdo* by Annie Detrick © 2009. Used with permission

themselves. It was an affirmation of resilience and strength. In the nineteenth century this caused great concern to the military police of the states of Rio de Janeiro and Bahia, and for several years the practice of capoeira was considered illegal. In the twentieth century, it morphed into a choreographic game, a type of martial arts, or a dance, and has gained popularity among not only African descendants but among all Brazilians. Capoeira requires more dexterity and subtlety than brute strength and utilizes skilled acrobatic movements of the legs and the feet.

Nowadays, capoeira is one of the most popular tourist attractions of Bahia and has gained a more playful character. It has also assimilated movements of jujitsu and boxing. There are several different schools of capoeira. The most famous is capoeira de Angola, and the others derive from it—Angolinha and jogo de fora, to name a few. Although there are small differences in each of these styles, capoeira is never performed without music.

Part of the capoeira training routine is learning to sing the songs and play these on traditional Brazilian instruments: *berimbau* (a one-stringed, bowed instrument played with a stick and a stone), *ganzá* (shaker), *pandeiro* (shallow frame drum with jingles, similar to our tambourine), and the *caxixi* (pronounced "kah-shee-shee"; a shaker made of wicker), which accompanies the *berimbau* (figure 1.4).

Lined up in a *roda* (circle), a soloist chants the call and the group responds with a small refrain. The music usually starts slowly and then gets faster as the *capoeiristas* (those who practice capoeira) warm up their bodies. Music functions as an energy catapult for the *capoeiristas* and its repetitive characteristics have a hypnotic effect, leading some performers into a state of trance.

FIGURE 1.3.   Pen and Ink *Capoeiristas* by Annie Detrick © 2009. Used with permission

The dance recently has become highly popular and is performed by people from all over the world. *Capoeiristas* undergo rigorous physical training and develop strong and fit bodies. Presently, several gyms around the world

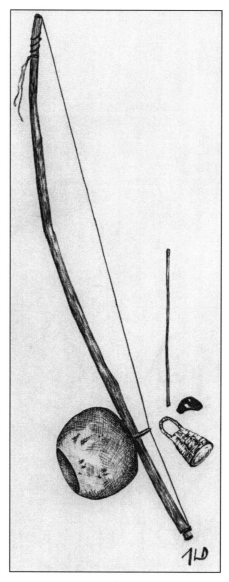

FIGURE 1.4.   Pen and Ink *Berimbau* by Annie Detrick © 2009. Used with permission

offer capoeira as an effective workout routine. When you observe a *roda de capoeira* (capoeira circle) you will notice that before the participants gather in a roda, they begin their routine with intensive physical conditioning. For more information, check YouTube for videos from Abadá Capoeira, or visit www.abadacapoeira.com/html/home.shtml. A popular capoeira chant is "Paranauê."

Portuguese: *Paranauê, paranauê, paraná*

Portuguese: *Eu vou dizer ao meu senhor que a manteiga derramou*

IPA: *[ew vow dʒiˈze aw mew siˈŋo kiˈa mãˈtejga dexaˈmow]*

Translation: *I am going to tell my master that the butter has melted*

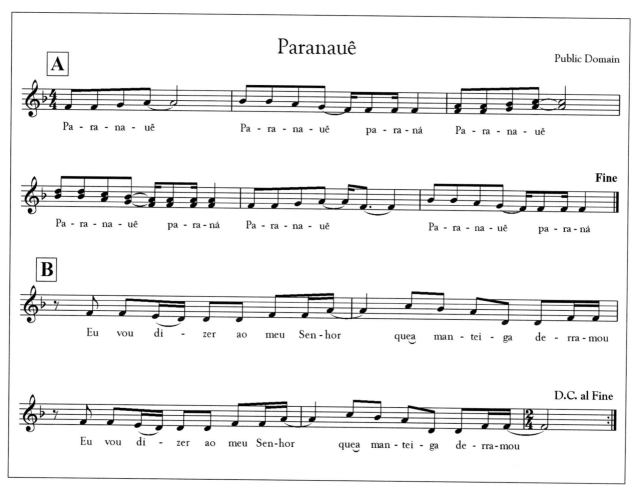

FIGURE 1.5.   "Paranauê"

Learning Outcomes:

Students are able to sing the melody of "Os Escravos de Jó" in Portuguese.

Students successfully play the passing game while singing "Os Escravos de Jó" accurately, transferring the visual spatial pattern in the game to their own hand movements.

Students successfully memorize the movement sequences of the passing game.

Students perform the song "Os Escravos de Jó" accompanied by short rhythmic ostinati played on Brazilian instruments.

Students are able to correctly identify the traditional Brazilian instruments introduced in this lesson on worksheet 1.

Students, divided into groups, perform their choreographed dance movements in the style of capoeira.

Students demonstrate basic knowledge of capoeira by completing worksheet 2.

Worksheet 1: Brazilian Musical Instruments and Their Function in Capoeira

Berimbau

Caxixi

Pandeiro

Ganzá

Worksheet 2: Understanding the Social and Musical Function of Capoeira

Country of origin

Musical elements

Where and how it is performed

Social and cultural meanings

Why was capoeira illegal in the nineteenth century?

What role does capoeira have today in Brazil and in the world?

Extensions

Because folk songs are transmitted orally, there are usually several versions of the same song. Although the music transcription and game instructions are based on the Brazilian tradition, this folk song "Os Escravos de Jó" has been claimed by several other cultures. The teacher can teach the version found in Choksy and Brummit's (1987) *120 Singing Games and Dances for Elementary Schools*. According to the authors, the song is played in Calgary, Canada, and by Hispanic children in California ("Al Citron"). It would be educational and interesting to discuss the oral tradition, and how these two versions are similar or different.

Another possible extension is to compare and contrast the movements of capoeira with the ones from break dancing, analyzing the similarities and differences between the African influences in Brazil and the United States.

Additional Resources

Enciclopédia de Música Brasileira: Popular, Erudita, e Folclórica [Encyclopedia of Brazilian music: Popular, classic, and folk] (1998).

Sabanovich, D. (2004). *Brazilian Percussion Manual: Rhythms and Techniques with Application for the Drum Set.*

RHYTHMS AND PROVERBS: WINDOWS TO THE CULTURES OF AFRICA AND LATIN AMERICA

National Standards

Music

Standard 1: Singing, alone and with others, a varied repertoire of music

Standard 2: Performing on instruments, alone and with others, a varied repertoire of music

Standard 6: Listening to, analyzing, and describing music

Standard 7: Evaluating music and music performances

Standard 8: Understanding relationships between music, the other arts, and disciplines outside the arts

Standard 9: Understanding music in relation to history and culture

In collaboration with the English language arts teacher or alone, the music teacher may also address NCTE/IRA Standards for English Language Arts 1, 2, 3, 4, and 9. They are available at www.ncte.org/standards.

Objectives

Students will sing, accurately and on pitch, a pentatonic melody.

Students will demonstrate knowledge of pitch relationships through use of the Curwen hand signs and solfa singing.

Students will perform in C pentatonic on the soprano xylophone (SX).

Students will accurately perform rhythmic ostinati and accompaniment on pitched and nonpitched percussion, and the recorder.

Students will perform in a class ensemble.

Students will demonstrate knowledge of "proverbs" through a collaborative, dramatic presentation.

Students will respond to musical form through musical and dramatic performance.

Materials

Instruments

Soprano recorders

Soprano xylophones—the melody played on the soprano xylophone can also be played on the *kalimba* (thumb piano)

Bass xylophones (or boom whackers)

Cowbell (or *agogô* bells)

Claves

Conga drums

Props

World map

Proverb cards (one proverb, from Africa or Latin America, is written on each card)

Colorful scarves, flowers, baskets, and other items for dramatization

"Traveling Song" (figure 1.19)

Other Resources

Anderson, W. M., and P. S. Campbell. (1996). *Multicultural Perspectives in Music Education*

Brian, A. (1999). *The Night Has Ears: African Proverbs*

Campbell, P. S. (2004). *Teaching Music Globally: Experiencing Music, Expressing Culture*

"Proverbs" lesson plan from the ReadWriteThink website: www.readwritethink.org/lessons/lesson_view
.asp?id=184

Quesada, R. (1998). *When the Road Is Long, Even Slippers Feel Tight: A Collection of Latin American Proverbs*

Wade, B. C. (2004). *Thinking Musically: Experiencing Music, Expressing Culture*

Zona, G. A. (1994). *The Soul Would Have No Rainbow If the Eyes Had No Tears and Other Native American Proverbs*

Process

Part I: A Section

1. Teacher sings the melody of "Traveling Song" (shown in figure 1.6), using Curwen hand signs.

FIGURE 1.6. "Traveling Song"

FIGURE 1.7. Travel On

2. Teacher sings the melody of "Traveling Song" again, and asks students to identify the highest and lowest pitches, in solfa (*la* and *la₁*).

3. Students sing the song in solfa, using hand signs, while the teacher models the hand signs.

4. Teacher sings song with text; students echo phrase by phrase.

5. Students sing the song, while teacher plays the recorder ostinato shown in figure 1.8.

6. Teacher plays the recorder ostinato, asking students to identify which pitches are being played in solfa (*sol* and *la*). Teacher then asks students to identify the pitch names (G and A).

7. Students play the recorder ostinato while teacher sings (students may think the words "travel on and on").

8. Teacher will divide the class in two groups. One group sings while the other plays recorder ostinato, and then they switch.

9. Teacher asks students to move to the barred instruments, and to set them up in C pentatonic (removing all of the F and B bars).

10. Teacher asks students to figure out the "Traveling Song" melody, giving students clues, such as "Which pitch is *do* in C pentatonic?" "Which note in solfa did we begin our song on?" "What is *sol* in C pentatonic?" Teacher should encourage students to help each other learn the melody without words as shown in figure 1.9.

11. Teacher patches an eighth note pulse, mirroring the bass xylophone part (BX) in figure 1.10, speaking "mo-vin', mo-vin', mo-vin' mo-vin'," and so on.

FIGURE 1.8.   "Traveling Song" Ostinato

FIGURE 1.9.   "Traveling Song" Melody

FIGURE 1.10.   Movin' On

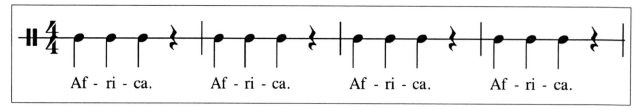

FIGURE 1.11.   Africa Rhythm

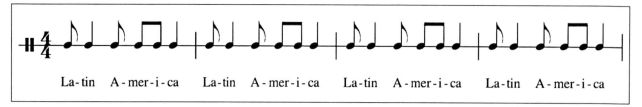

FIGURE 1.12.   Latin America Rhythm

12. Students echo, and mirror the movement, transferring it to the BX when ready.

13. Teacher sings and patches the AX (alto xylophone) part (figure 1.7, "Travel On").

14. Students mirror teacher by patching the AX part, and then transferring it to the AX when ready.

15. Teacher patches and speaks the conga part in figure 1.11.

16. Students echo and transfer to the conga when ready.

17. Teacher claps and speaks the clave part in figure 1.12.

18. Students echo and transfer to the claves when ready.

19. Teacher assigns each student to a part. An ensemble is created by layering in parts in the following order (see score): BX, conga, claves, AX, recorder, voice, and SX.

Part II: B Section

1. Teacher asks student to identify the places mentioned in the A section of the "Traveling Song" ensemble (Africa and Latin America).

2. Students locate each region on a world map, noting that Africa is a continent, while Latin America covers the continent of South America and part of North America.

3. Teacher engages students in a discussion of the music of each region. (Students may have studied the music of Africa and Latin America prior to this lesson, and will thus be able to create a chart of characteristics, similarities, and differences of their respective musics. If students have not studied the characteristics before, teacher may introduce them at this time. In this ensemble, the use of syncopation, layered rhythm patterns, the pentatonic scale, and instrument timbres are common to both cultures.)

4. Teacher speaks the first phrase of the B section text shown in figure 1.13; students echo. Repeat as needed.

5. Teacher speaks the second phrase of the B section text shown in figure 1.14; students echo. Repeat as needed.

6. Teacher asks students, "What is a proverb?" Students brainstorm possibilities, and also cite some proverbs they know.

7. Teacher lists characteristics of proverbs on the board, and leads discussion on the significance of proverbs,

FIGURE 1.13.   Mexico Ecuador

FIGURE 1.14.   Kenya Rwanda

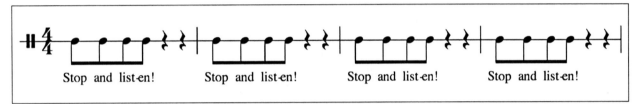

FIGURE 1.15.   Stop and Listen Rhythm

FIGURE 1.16.   Don't You Go Away Rhythm

what they can tell us about a culture, and how they can cross cultures (see "Proverb Definitions" at the end of this lesson plan). Teacher and students may also compare the characteristics of proverbs to folk music, such as both are passed in oral tradition, give insight into culture, have historical value, tell stories, and have survived the test of time.

8. Teacher patsches and speaks the conga part shown in figure 1.15. Students echo, and transfer to the conga when ready.

9. Teacher claps and speaks the clave part shown in figure 1.16. Students echo and transfer to the claves when ready.

10. Most students speak the B section text, while a few students are assigned to the conga and clave parts. An ensemble is created by layering in parts in the following order (see score): cowbell (played by teacher; see figure 1.17), conga, clave, voices.

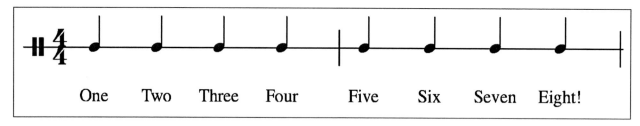

FIGURE 1.17.   One-Two

FIGURE 1.18.   Photograph of African People by James A. Cunningham © 2007. Used with permission

Part III: C Section

1. Teacher explains to students that they will be divided into small groups, with each group receiving a choice of proverbs to dramatize.
2. Teacher gives an example by choosing a student to help dramatize the West African proverb, "It takes a whole village to raise a child."
3. Teacher divides students into groups of approximately six people. Each group is given two proverb cards—one from Latin America, and one from Africa.

4. Students are instructed to read each card, discuss its meaning, and choose one to dramatize. Students may dramatize the proverb any way they want, as long as everyone participates. The proverb must be spoken at least once. This can be done within the dramatization, or before or after the dramatization. Students may use available props to aid in their dramatization.

5. Students rehearse their dramatizations, and perform for the class. The class discusses the possible meanings of each proverb.

Part IV: Putting It All Together!
The form of the activity "Travel On!" is as follows (assuming there are four groups of students):

A section

Interlude (cowbell part played by teacher)

B section

C section: group 1 performs proverb dramatization

A section

Interlude (cowbell part played by teacher)

B section

C section: group 2 performs proverb dramatization

Continue sequence until each group has performed

A section (ends the performance)

During the performance, there will always be two groups playing the instrument parts during the A and B section, while one group is getting ready to dramatize its proverb. The group that has just finished dramatizing its proverb will sing "Traveling Song" (full score shown in figure 1.19) and will speak the text of the B section. A rotation may be set up as shown in figure 1.20.

For a public performance, teacher may want to assign specific instrument parts to each student (or students can decide among themselves within each group). In the classroom, all students will know each part, and should be able to fill in the parts as needed.

Learning Outcomes
Assessment is based on the ability of students to sing and play accurately, their ability to work cooperatively with others in an ensemble and in small groups, and their success at capturing the meaning of proverbs in dramatic performance. Teacher may want to digitally record a final performance so that students can evaluate themselves.

Traveling Song

D. Cunningham

2004, 2008

FIGURE 1.19.   "Traveling Song" Score

FIGURE 1.19. "Traveling Song" Score

FIGURE 1.19. "Traveling Song" Score

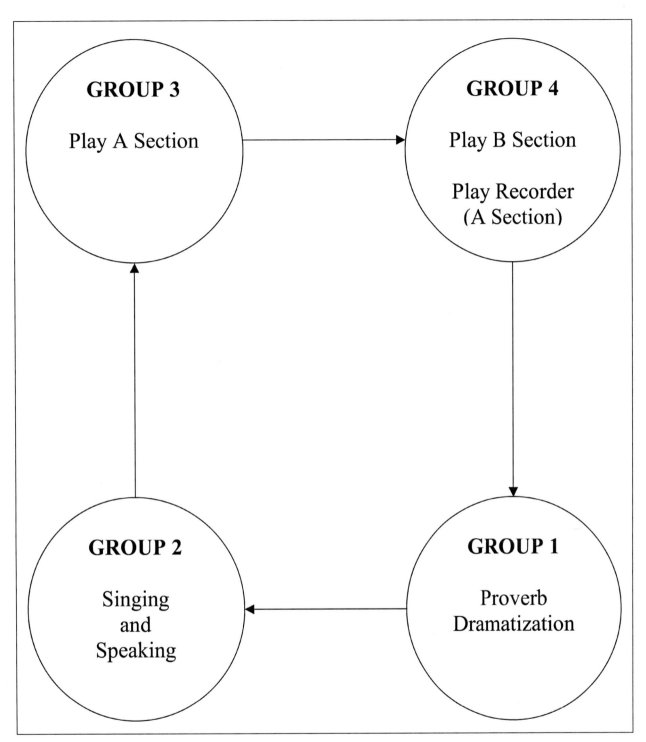

FIGURE 1.20. Performance Diagram

Group Work Assessment Rubric

Group Members:

1._____

2._____

3._____

4._____

5._____

6._____

Group members worked well together	3	2	1
All group members performed their parts accurately	3	2	1
Group performance showed creativity	3	2	1
Overall performance captured the meaning of the proverb	3	2	1
All group members demonstrated appropriate audience behavior	3	2	1

Total possible = 15

Group total = _____

Rhythms and Proverbs Self-Assessment Rubric

Name:_____

1. I performed each instrument part accurately and musically with the ensemble.	3	2	1
2. I performed my part accurately and musically within the ensemble.	3	2	1
3. I can give examples of proverbs from my own or other cultures.	3	2	1

Total Possible = 9

Total:_____

ReadWriteThink.org (a website developed by the International Reading Association and the National Council of Teachers of English) provides a handout on proverbs.

Proverb Definitions

Proverbs are popular sayings which contain advice or state a generally accepted truth. Because most proverbs have their origins in oral tradition, they are generally worded in such a way as to be remembered easily and tend to change little from generation to generation, so much so that sometimes their specific meaning is no longer relevant. For instance, the proverb "penny wise, pound foolish" is a holdover from when America was a British colony and used the pound as currency. Proverbs function as "folk wisdom," general advice about how to act and live. And because they are folk wisdom, they strongly reflect the cultural values and physical environment from which they arise. For instance, island cultures such as Hawaii have proverbs about the sea. Eastern cultures have proverbs about elephants, and American proverbs, many collected and published by Benjamin Franklin, are about hard work bringing success. Proverbs are used to support arguments, to provide lessons and instruction, and to stress shared values.

Proverbs are not clichés

Clichés are widely used, even overused, phrases that are often metaphorical in nature. Clichés often have their origins in literature, television, or movies rather than in folk tradition.

Some Common Features of Proverbs

Proverbs are passed down through time with little change in form. Proverbs are often used metaphorically and it is in understanding their metaphorical nature that we can unravel their meaning. While "a stitch in time saves nine," "don't count your chickens before they've hatched," and "don't throw the baby out with the bathwater" are common proverbs, few of us stitch clothes, count chickens, or throw out bathwater. Proverbs often make use of grammatical and rhetorical devices that help make them memorable, including alliteration, rhyme, parallel structure, repetition of key words or phrases, and strong imagery.

Some Common Proverbs

Look before you leap.

Don't throw out the baby with the bathwater.

Where there's a will, there's a way.

All's well that ends well.

Don't count your chickens before they've hatched.

If it looks like a duck, walks like a duck, and quacks like a duck, it is a duck.

A stitch in time saves nine.

Some Common Clichés

She was white as a sheet.

The tension was so thick you could cut it like butter.

He stood as still as a deer in the headlights.

I'm as fit as a fiddle.

You could read her like an open book.

FANTASTIC FABLES: EXPLORING NATIVE AMERICAN CULTURE

National Standards

Music

Standard 8: Understanding relationships between music, the other arts, and disciplines outside the arts

Standard 9: Understanding music in relation to history and culture

If working in collaboration with the English teacher or alone, this lesson may also address National Standards for English Language Arts 1, 2, 3, and 11. These are available at www.ncte.org/standards.

Prior Knowledge

Prior to this lesson, students should have had opportunities to explore Native American culture, including but not limited to the importance of nature, spirituality, and balance among all things. They should also have had opportunities to discover the elements of a fable, including but not limited to allegory, personification, moral content (lesson learned), and main character traits.

Objectives

Students will use prior knowledge to construct a graphic organizer displaying general characteristics of Native American culture.

Students will use prior knowledge to complete a graphic organizer outlining the elements of a fable.

Students will identify specific elements of a fable found in Ray Buckley's book, *The Wing*.

Students will identify specific examples of the characteristics of Native American culture found in *The Wing*.

Students will demonstrate understanding of the fable through written and oral responses to questions related to content posed by the teacher.

Students will explore the use of song in the fable, and make connections between musical function and Native American culture through teacher-directed questions, written reflection, and discussion.

Materials

Buckley, R. (2002). *The Wing*

Burton, B. (1993). *Moving within the Circle*

Fable elements graphic organizer

Large chart paper

 "Meaning of Music" questions

Native American characteristics graphic organizer

The Wing content chart

The Wing reflection questions

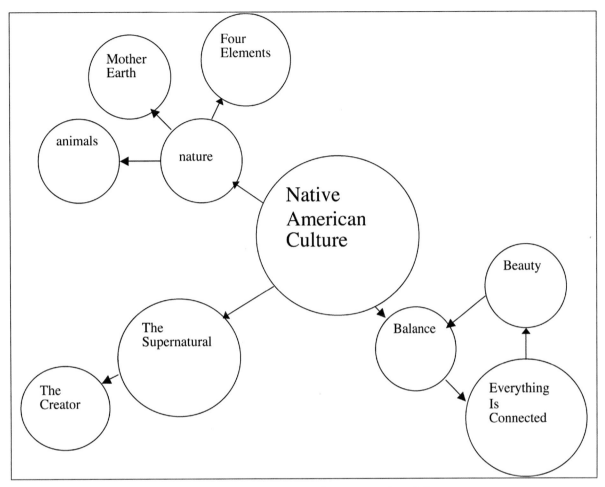

FIGURE 1.21.   Characteristics of Native American Culture

Process

Part I

1. Teacher divides the class into four small groups. Two groups will work with the topic "Characteristics of Native American Culture" using the chart in figure 1.21, and two groups will work with the topic "Elements of a Fable," using the chart in figure 1.22.
2. Teacher instructs groups of students to brainstorm on their given topics, creating and completing the graphic organizers.
3. Teacher combines like groups to compare their graphic organizers, creating one on large chart paper to be shared with the class.
4. Students present their work to the class; the class fills in any "missing" information.

Part II

1. Teacher reads the fable *The Wing* to the class. The class is seated in a circle, representing the Native American concept of connectedness. The teacher asks the class to be thinking about the elements of a fable and the characteristics of Native American culture as they listen.

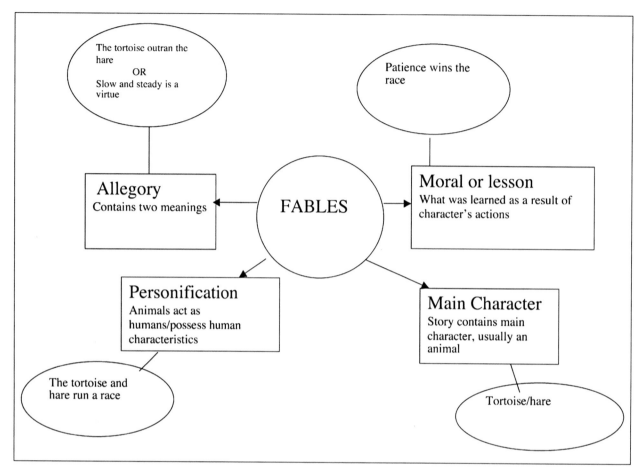

FIGURE 1.22.   Fable Graphic Organizer

2. Students identify the specific elements of a fable as well as the specific characteristics of Native American culture as found in the fable, using *The Wing* content chart shown in figure 1.23.

3. Students share their answers in a class discussion format.

4. Students answer questions about the fable:

> How did "She Who Flies Swiftly" get her name?
> How did her broken wing affect her feeling of self-worth?
> How was "She Who Flies Swiftly" transformed?
> What acted as a catalyst for this transformation? In what way?
> What was her named changed to?
> If possible, share an experience that you or someone you know had that in some way created a "transformation."

5. Students share their answers in a class discussion format.

6. Teacher provides students with factual information about the function of music in Native American culture, and asks students to explore ways the use of song in the fable is indicative of the culture. Students use the "Meaning of Music" questions (shown below) to complete the activity. Students share their ideas with a partner.

7. Students share their ideas in a class discussion.

In the space provided, give examples of the elements of a fable and characteristics of Native American culture as read in the story *The Wing*, by Ray Buckley.

Fable	Main Character	Personification	Allegory	Moral/Lesson
The Wing				

Native American Culture	The Creator Was the creator or spiritual force reference in the text?	Nature How was it present in the fable?	Balance How was it achieved/restored?

FIGURE 1.23. *The Wing* Content Chart

Meaning of Music

Read the following narrative and answer the questions below.

According to Native American scholar Bryan Burton:

Native Americans consider music to be a gift from the Creator. All music is part of the Universe and individuals are allowed by the Creator to "catch" a song from this source. Music might be the product of an individual within a tribe or the result of a communal effort. Generally, music among the Native Americans has been considered functional. Music serves to join the natural with the supernatural, the person with the Creator. Songs and dances contain spiritual powers, which can help bring about a desired effect. The performers, both singers and dancers, serve to create the functional purpose of the music. (*Moving within the Circle*, Bryan Burton [Danbury, CT: World Music Press, 1993], p. 22)

How is the use of song in this fable typical of Native American culture?

What is its meaning?

Learning Outcomes

Students are evaluated on written work done in class and/or as homework.

Students are evaluated on the basis of their contributions to class discussion.

Teacher reads another Native American fable to the class, and students identify the elements of a fable and Native American characteristics using a content chart similar to the one used for *The Wing*.

Extension

Future lessons may include reading more fables, writing own fables, comparing fables of different cultures, listening to and performing Native American music and dance, analyzing Native American music and dance as it connects to history and culture, and exploring the use of music/song in fables of other cultures.

2

Music and Science

THE LIFE OF A SNOWFLAKE: EXPLORING HEXACHORDS, HEXAGONS, AND THE WATER CYCLE

National Standards

Music

Standard 1: Singing, alone and with others, a varied repertoire of music

Standard 2: Performing on instruments, alone and with others, a varied repertoire of music

Standard 3: Improvising melodies, variations, and accompaniments

Standard 8: Understanding relationships between music, the other arts, and disciplines outside the arts

In collaboration with the science teacher or alone, the teacher may address Content Standard D for Earth and Space Science, available at www.nap.edu/readingroom/books/nses/6d.html#csa58.

Objectives

Students will explore the movement of forces in nature through kinesthetic experimentation.

Students will sing expressively within a given hexachord.

Students will improvise within a given hexachord (*do–re–mi–fa–sol–la*).

Students will accompany a song and dramatic presentation using barred instruments.

Students will use prior knowledge to review the water cycle process.

Students will demonstrate knowledge of snowflake formation and the water cycle using dramatic expression.

Materials

A classroom set of paper snowflakes created using a hexagonal structure (six branches each, with no two the same); see http://highhopes.com/snowflakes.html for instructions

Hydrogen/oxygen visual aid: a model of the molecular structure of a snowflake can be created by using six Styrofoam balls to represent oxygen atoms and six pipe cleaners to represent hydrogen atoms

"Snow Song"

Barred instruments (Orff instrumentarium, if possible)

Nonpitched percussion instruments, including a hand drum

Colorful scarves and/or other props

Internet access

Digital recorder

Classroom performance rubric

Water cycle quiz

Process

Part I

1. Teacher instructs students to silently move around the room to the beat of the drum. When the drumbeat stops, students should freeze in the position of _____. (Teacher inserts a variety of themes here, such as favorite winter activity, something found in the winter, and so on.)
2. Teacher instructs students that they will hear music (improvised by teacher within a C hexachord), and should move around the room as if they are _____ (wind, rain, etc.). Students are no longer restricted by the beat—movement is free.
3. Teacher then instructs students to move as if they are snowflakes. Teacher plays the bass metallophone (BM) part and sings the "Snow Song" as students move, freezing in place when the music stops.
4. Teacher chooses student leaders, asking the class to "move like X moves" and so forth.

Part II

1. Teacher gives each student a paper snowflake, instructing students to continue silently moving like snowflakes, looking for another person who has a matching snowflake. Teacher continues to play and sing "Snow Song."
2. Teacher stops after a few times through the song. Students will not have (or should not have) found partners, as none of the snowflakes are the same. The teacher asks students why they could not find partners, and leads them in a discussion about the uniqueness of snowflakes.
3. Teacher asks students why/how snowflakes form (students may or may not know the correct answers at this point).
4. Teacher asks students to count how many branches or sides their paper snowflakes have (six), and then asks students to identify what we call a shape that has six sides (hexagon).
5. Teacher leads students in a discussion about the hexagonal shape of snow crystals, explaining how they are formed and how some grow "branches." Teacher may use the hydrogen/oxygen visual aid at this point, as well as the website www.snowcrystals.com.
6. Students recall the water cycle, reviewing it through class discussion. Teacher may draw a diagram on the board and review the terms *evaporation, transpiration, water vapor, condensation, precipitation,* and *infiltration* in this way:

The sun heats the water on the earth.

The water becomes a gas, or "vapor" (water vapor), which is absorbed into the air (evaporation).

Plants give off water vapor to release waste (transpiration). This also evaporates into the air.

The air holds the water vapor until it becomes too cold to hold all of it, at which time some of it condenses (condensation), forming water droplets that collect into clouds.

If a cloud is blown upward or into a colder air mass, more water will condense, and be released in the form of rain, hail, sleet, or snow, depending on the temperature of the air mass (precipitation).

If a cloud is cold enough, the water droplets freeze, each one becoming a particle of ice.

An ice particle/crystal grows when the water vapor surrounding it condenses onto its surface, creating a snowflake.

The water vapor molecules are made up of two parts hydrogen and one part oxygen (use visual). When the molecules freeze to form an ice crystal, they begin as a prism in the shape of a hexagon. When water vapor condenses onto the ice crystal, it attaches to each of the six points on the hexagon, creating branches.

The water that is released from the clouds (precipitation) returns to the earth and is absorbed into the soil (infiltration). Some is used to help plants grow, and the rest is released into the air, as the water cycle continues.

7. Teacher may show students pictures of various types of snowflakes, as found in the books listed under "Extensions," or at www.snowcrystals.com.

Part III

1. Teacher sings "Snow Song" and asks students to identify how many times they hear the phrase "snow is falling down" (three times—it happens first, so it is the "a" phrase).
2. Students echo-sing the "a" phrase, then sing it within the song while teacher sings the "b" phrase.
3. Students echo-sing the "b" phrase, then sing it within the song while teacher sings the "a" phrase.
4. Students sing entire song.
5. Students move to barred instruments and remove the B bars.
6. Teacher asks students to play the "a" phrase, starting on G. Students note that the notes are right next to each other, and move down.
7. Teacher asks students to listen to the "b" phrase in relation to the "a" phrase, and figure out which note it starts on (G—the same note the "a" phrase started on).
8. Teacher breaks the "b" phrase into two parts. Teacher asks students to show the melodic contour of "swirling all around" with their arms, noting that most of the time it stays on one note, then moves up and back down.
9. Students play "swirling all around."
10. Teacher and students repeat the process with the rest of the "b" phrase, noting that it does not start on G, mostly moves down, but ends by going up a step to D.
11. Students play "covering the ground," and then connect both parts of the "b" phrase.
12. Students play melody of whole song; teacher plays the BM part to accompany.
13. Teacher models the alto metallophone (AM) part, singing absolute pitch names.
14. Students sing the melody.
15. Teacher asks students when the AM plays in relation to the text (comes in on "down").
16. Teacher and students sing, playing the AM part at the appropriate time.
17. Students sing and play the AM part while teacher adds the wind chimes (WC) at the appropriate time.
18. Teacher asks students to identify when the WC played in relation to the AM.

19. Teacher chooses students to play the WC, only during the "a" phrase.
20. Teacher chooses students to play the contra bass bar (CBB), instructing them to play on the downbeat throughout the piece, being careful to count six beats during the "b" section.

Part IV

1. Students and teacher list known rhythmic patterns in simple meter (make separate columns for one-beat and two-beat patterns).
2. Teacher asks students to brainstorm words and ideas that have to do with snow—such as what we wear, what we eat, how we feel, and what we see.
3. Students clap and speak each word or phrase, noting how many syllables each word receives, and where the syllabic stress falls.
4. Teacher instructs students to create word chains containing six beats each (said with appropriate syllabic stress), remembering that a snowflake has six branches (for example, "snowmen–play outside–icy storm").
5. Students share with the class while teacher writes suggestions on the board. Teacher instructs students to try to create word patterns that make sense, and that will be easy to remember.
6. Teacher instructs students to improvise a melody on a barred instrument, using one of the word chains from the board. Students will use the hexachord C–D–E–F–G–A for this activity, and should remove all the B bars from their instruments. Teacher points out the prefix "hexa," noting that it can refer to many things made up of "sixes."
7. After students have had time to improvise, some students share their ideas by performing for the class.
8. Students choose the patterns they like the best, and teacher or students write the pitch names below the rhythmic notation on the board, as shown in figure 2.1.
9. All students play the patterns written on the board. Class decides which instrument will play which pattern.
10. Students play or sing "Snow Song," shown in figure 2.2, which is now the A section of a larger form. Students play their word chains from the board, which now become the B section of a larger form, and then end by repeating the A section. Note that the BM part now has six beats. Allow students to decide how many times each pattern will be played, and when each pattern will be played (simultaneously, one after the other, etc.).

Part V

1. Teacher breaks students into small groups and tells them that they are going to dramatize the life cycle of a snowflake.
2. Teacher asks students to identify the main "characters" in the water cycle, such as the sun, water, water vapor, clouds, and snow crystals with six branches.
3. Teacher asks students to decide what each character should do, how it should do it, what props/instruments to use, and so on. Teacher may need to give students time to work informally on creative movement/acting.
4. Teacher or students decide who will act out the water cycle, and who will play the instrumental accompaniment.

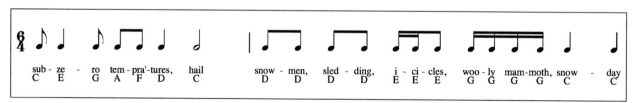

FIGURE 2.1. Six-Beat Chain

Snow Song

D. Cunningham

©2006

FIGURE 2.2. "Snow Song"

Snow Song

FIGURE 2.2. "Snow Song"

Snow Song   3

FIGURE 2.2.   "Snow Song"

5. Students perform the piece using the following form: A—"Snow Song," A section (instruments and voices); B—"Snow Song," B section, played underneath the dramatic presentation of the water cycle; and A—"Snow Song," A section.

Learning Outcomes

Students sing expressively using appropriate phrasing and intonation, as rehearsed in class.

Students demonstrate the ability to improvise within a hexachord using word chains.

Students create six-beat patterns using known rhythms.

Through musical performance, students demonstrate the ability to shift between meter in 4 and meter in 6.

Students perform as an ensemble and demonstrate the ability to maintain a steady beat, use appropriate dynamics, and make smooth transitions between sections.

Students appropriately and creatively respond to music through movement.

Through dramatic performance, students clearly demonstrate the water cycle process.

Students use appropriate vocabulary words to describe the water cycle, as well as snowflake formation.

Assessment Tools

Digitally record the classroom performance. Watch it as a class and have each student assess the class using the performance assessment rubric.

Distribute and evaluate the water cycle quiz.

Classroom Performance Assessment Rubric

Directions: Please carefully watch and listen to the digital recording of our class performance, and rate it using each of the following items, with 3 being the highest score possible for each item.

1. We sang "Snow Song" expressively by using energy and appropriate phrasing, and
   by singing in tune.   3   2   1
2. In our ensemble we kept the tempo steady.   3   2   1
3. In our instrumental ensemble we used appropriate dynamics so that the singing
   could be heard.   3   2   1
4. As an ensemble, we made smooth transitions between each section of the
   performance.   3   2   1
5. When we acted out the water cycle, all the "characters" were represented.   3   2   1

Total: _____/15

Water Cycle Quiz

Fill in the blanks with words from the table below. You will use each word once.

1. _____ occurs when the sun heats up water on the earth's surface and it becomes a gas absorbed into the air.

2. _____ occurs when the water vapor in the air gets cold and changes back into liquid, forming water droplets that combine to become clouds.

3. _____ occurs when water returns to the ground and is either absorbed by plant roots or released into the air in the form of water vapor.

4. _____ occurs when clouds are blown into a colder air mass, causing more water droplets to form. The clouds cannot hold all the water, so they release it in the form of rain, hail, sleet or snow.

5. _____ are large collections of water droplets in the air.

6. _____ occurs when plants release waste into the air in the form of water vapor.

7. _____ is water in the form of gas.

8/9. _____ and _____ are the two types of atoms needed to form a water molecule (H_2O).

10. A _____ has six branches.

Hydrogen	Precipitation
Water vapor	Oxygen
Condensation	Evaporation
Clouds	Transpiration
Infiltration	Snowflake

Extensions
Other resources that might be helpful in extending this lesson include the following:

Cassino, M., and J. Nelson. (2009). *The Story of Snow: The Science of Winter's Wonder.*

Libbrecht, K. (2003). *The Snowflake: Winter's Secret Beauty.* Scientific facts about snowflakes, as well as beautiful color pictures of snowflakes.

Martin, J. B. (1998). *Snowflake Bentley.* Winner of the Caldecott Medal, children's biography of Wilson Bentley, the first scientist to successfully photograph snowflakes and document their characteristics.

Schafer, R. M. (1992). *Snowforms.* SSAA choral piece, with text consisting of Inuit words for snow. The score is printed on aqua-colored paper, and the notation is nontraditional—it actually looks like snow forms on paper.

Waldman, N. (2003). *The Snowflake.* Traces the life cycle of a snowflake from January to December.

www.snowcrystals.com. A very informative website with answers to many questions about snowflake formation. This site is by the author of *The Snowflake: Winter's Secret Beauty* and has many pictures also found in the book.

Extensions/Modifications for the Non-Music Educator
There are many connections that the science educator can make using the water cycle, the formation of crystals, and molecular structures. There are many "experiments" that can be done with snowflakes, including catching and preserving them, and creating them. These projects can be found on websites and in science experiment books.

Math and geometry educators can work with the hexagon and explore further, including finding the area, angles, and lines of symmetry.

Extensions for the Music Educator
Musically, one can further explore the use of hexachords and hexatonic patterns. An interesting juxtaposition would be to explore the whole-tone scale (which has six tones) and the hexagonal structure of snowflakes, and the symmetry inherent in each. This lesson could also be used to introduce *fa*, as the hexachord moves out of the pentatonic realm with the addition of *fa*. Create a model of the hexagonal structure of a snowflake by using pipe cleaners to represent the hydrogen atoms and Styrofoam balls to represent the oxygen atoms, as shown in figure 2.3.

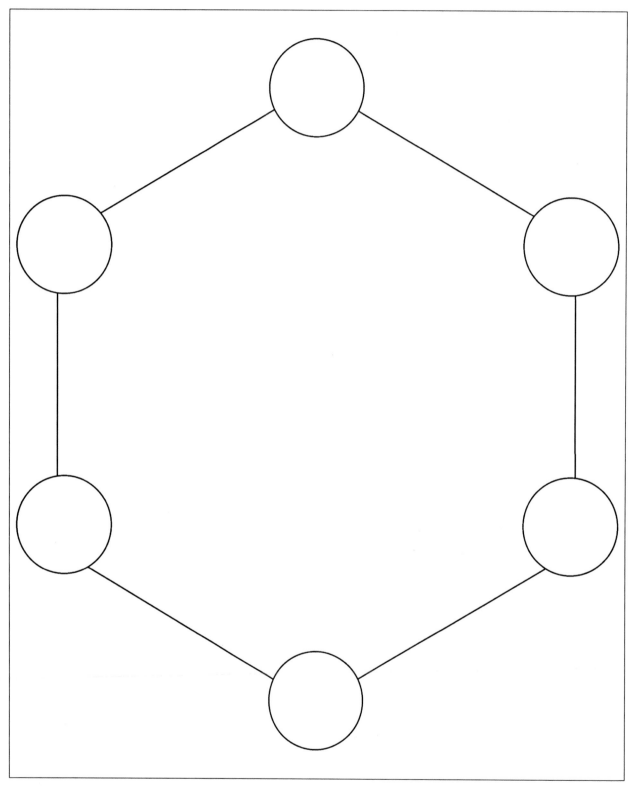

FIGURE 2.3. Snow Hexagon

BUTTERFLIES

National Standards

Music

Standard 1: Singing, alone and with others, a varied repertoire of music

Standard 6: Listening to, analyzing, and describing music

Standard 7: Evaluating music and music performances

Standard 8: Understanding relationships between music, the other arts, and disciplines outside the arts

Standard 9: Understanding music in relation to history and culture

In collaboration with the social studies teacher or alone, the music teacher may also address social studies standards, such as New York State Social Studies Standard 3, available from www.emsc.nysed.gov/ciai/standards.

NCTE/IRA English Language Arts Standard 1 and Standard 2 can also be addressed in collaboration with the English language arts teacher or alone. The standards are available at www.ncte.org/standards.

Objectives

Part I

Students will understand and learn about the geography of Brazil with the help of a map.

Students will understand the seasons of Brazil's tropical weather.

Students will learn a Brazilian folk song in Portuguese (or use the optional English words).

Students will compare and contrast the seasons of the United States and Brazil during the December holidays.

Students will compose a melodic descant for the song "Borboleta Pequenina" and will perform it in Portuguese or English.

Part II

Students will be introduced to some of the events of the Holocaust through poetry and music.

Students will read and write for information and understanding about events of the Holocaust.

Students will analyze and describe how the text of "At Terezín" was set to music.

Students will set to music a poem of their choice from . . . *I Never Saw Another Butterfly* . . .

Materials

Map of South America and Brazil, or computer with Internet access (map available at www.worldatlas.com/webimage/countrys/samerica/br.htm)

Colorful pictures of butterflies from the Internet or from Oceana Books (2007). *Butterflies: A Fascinating Guide to This Beautiful Insect Species*

Volavková, H. (1993). . . . *I Never Saw Another Butterfly . . .: Children's Drawings and Poems from Terezín Concentration Camp, 1942–1944*

Brazilian folk song, "Borboleta Pequenina" (Little Butterfly)

Recordings and sheet music for R. Convery (1991). "At Terezín"

Tropical Rainforest DVD

"Butterflies and Moths" guide, www.flmnh.ufl.edu/education/guides/butterfly-guide.pdf

Process

Part I

1. Teacher introduces the map of South America and highlights Brazil, focusing on Brazilian geography and teaching about its five regions: Northeast, North, South, Southwest, and Central West.
2. Teacher reviews the geography of the United States using a map.
3. Teacher introduces Brazil's tropical climate and draws comparisons with the seasons experienced in the United States.
4. Teacher teaches students about tropical butterflies using the "Butterflies and Moths" guide available at www.flmnh.ufl.edu/education/guides/butterfly-guide.pdf, which is accurate and readily accessible. Teacher may also use the Oceana book or any other resource on butterflies as a reference.

    Butterflies are insects from the order Lepidoptera, which means "scaly winged" (in Greek, *lepidos* means "scales," and *pteron* means "wings"). When closely examined, butterflies have really colorful tiny scales on their wings that look like fine powder. A person who studies butterflies is called a *lepidopterist*. A biologist who specializes in insects in general is called an *entomologist*.

    Some butterflies indigenous to Brazil are as follows:

Phoebis philea (Pieridae), commonly known as Orange-Barred Sulphur or Yellow Apricot, is bright yellow and loves gardens, parks, and road edges. Butterflies in this family have no tails and get their names from their colors, which are usually white, yellow, or orange.

Caligo memnon (Nymphalidae), commonly known as the Owl Butterfly, is one of Amazonia's largest species. It feeds on banana plants.

Morpho rhetenor (Nymphalidae), commonly known as Blue Morpho, has brilliant blue wings and lives in the rain forests of Brazil, Costa Rica, and Venezuela. Adult butterflies like to drink the juices of rotting fruits.

Pierella rhea (Nymphalidae) has two distinct shapes and colors for the forewings and hind wings. It flies in various countries within the Amazon forest. Nymphalidae is the largest family of butterflies with approximately five thousand species, such as Monarchs, Browns, and Riodinids.

5. Students choose colorful scarves that might represent the colors that they would like to see in a butterfly. Students verbally explain to their peers their reasons for choosing certain colors.
6. Teacher teaches the song "Borboleta Pequenina" (Little Butterfly) in Portuguese, shown in figure 2.4.
7. Teacher discusses the musical form of "Borboleta Pequenina": A(1–5) B(6–9) A(10–13) B(14–17) A(18–21).
8. Teacher explains the meaning of the Portuguese words, reminding the students that during the December

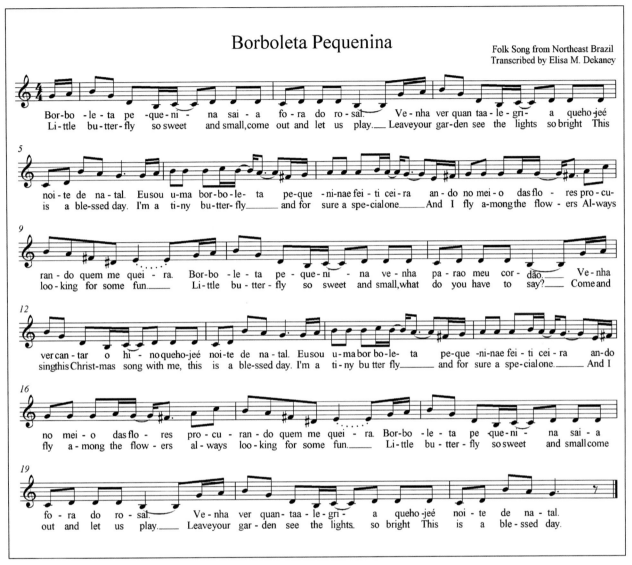

FIGURE 2.4. "Borboleta Pequenina"

holidays it is summer in Brazil and there are plenty of butterflies flying around and pollinating the plants. The weather in December is hot and humid throughout most of the country.

9. Students perform the song and use the colorful scarves while moving around the classroom pretending to be butterflies.

Part II

1. Teacher selects two poems, "The Butterfly" and "At Terezín," published in the book . . . *I Never Saw Another Butterfly . . .: Children's Drawings and Poems from Terezín Concentration Camp, 1942–1944.*

2. Teacher provides students with background information on children and the Holocaust. The information may be retrieved from the U.S. Holocaust Memorial Museum website (www.ushmm.org) or it can be based on the fore-

word of the book . . . *I Never Saw Another Butterfly* . . . which explains the origins of the ghetto Theresienstadt, or Terezín, located in Czechoslovakia. Terezín opened in October 1941; was liberated on May 8, 1945, by the Soviet army; and was closed on August 17, 1945. Numerous artists, musicians, and children were incarcerated in Terezín and several other concentration camps because of Nazi Germany's racial discrimination ideology and policies based on the hatred of Jews, or anti-Semitism. Communists, Sinti-Roma families (also known as Gypsies), persons with disabilities, Afro-Germans, and homosexuals were also persecuted, arrested, deported, and murdered by the Nazis.

3. After a thoughtful and detailed explanation of Terezín, teacher divides the class into small groups of four students each. Each group will read "The Butterfly" and "At Terezín" poems and consider the following questions:

What would it be like to be a child in a concentration camp?

How hard would it be to leave behind your house and everything that you owned?

What kinds of things would you have to do if you had to live without your parents or siblings?

Why do you think the title of the book is . . . *I Never Saw Another Butterfly* . . .?

What kinds of thoughts and feelings might we experience when we see butterflies?

What other questions come to your mind when you read this poem?

4. After students have had enough time to read and comprehend the poems, the teacher instructs students to share their thoughts and questions with each other.
5. Students actively listen to "At Terezín" by Robert Convery. Soon after, they explain in writing how the composer's musical ideas convey the meaning of the poem.
6. Students return to their small groups of four and select a poem from . . . *I Never Saw Another Butterfly* . . . and set it to music. There are no guidelines for the composition. Students should be able to work freely. Although there is a text, the song does not need to be a vocal composition.
7. Each small group of four will perform the song for the whole class.

Learning Outcomes

Part I

Students are able to successfully locate Brazil on the South American map, especially the Amazon forest, which is the home to several species of butterflies.

Students are able to identify the form of the song "Borboleta Pequenina" and perform it accompanied by body movements.

For homework, students will search the World Wide Web for pictures of Brazilian butterflies. They will prepare a short PowerPoint presentation for the next class and explain specific characteristics of the chosen butterfly.

Part II

Students are able to discuss in small groups their perceptions, thoughts, and ideas about life in the Terezín ghetto that they gathered from the poems "The Butterfly" and "At Terezín."

Students are able to express in writing some of the most important events related to the Holocaust and Terezín.

Students are able to verbally identify certain compositional choices Robert Convery made while setting the poem "At Terezín" to music.

Students demonstrate their understanding of some issues children faced at the Terezín ghetto by setting to music a poem from . . . *I Never Saw Another Butterfly* . . .

Extension

A possible extension to this lesson is to compare and contrast the different types of butterflies found in the United States with the ones found in Brazil.

Additional Resources

Anti-Defamation League, USC Shoah Foundation Institute, and Yad Vashem. (2005). *Echoes and Reflections: A Multimedia Curriculum on the Holocaust.*

Polacco, P. (2000). *The Butterfly.*

3

Music and Social Studies

CAJUN CAPERS: INTRODUCTION TO CAJUN CULTURE

National Standards

Music

Standard 1: Singing, alone and with others, a varied repertoire of music

Standard 2: Performing on instruments, alone and with others, a varied repertoire of music

Standard 3: Improvising melodies, variations, and accompaniments

Standard 6: Listening to, analyzing, and describing music

Standard 8: Understanding relationships between music, the other arts, and disciplines outside the arts

Standard 9: Understanding music in relation to history and culture

In collaboration with a teacher of languages other than English or alone, it's possible to address ACTFL Foreign Language Standards 3 and 4, available at www.educationworld.com/standards/national/lang_arts/f_lang/k_12 .shtml#nl-fl.k-12.2.

In collaboration with a social studies teacher or alone, it's possible to address National Social Studies Geography Standards 1, 2, and 4, as well as U.S. History Standards 3 and 4, available at www.educationworld.com/standards/ national/soc_sci/index.shtml.

Objectives

Students will become familiar with French words by speaking and/or singing them.

Students will identify characteristics of Cajun culture and music.

Students will identify the state of Louisiana on a map of the United States.

Students will move in rhythm to Cajun music using a variation of the Cajun two-step.

Students will sing expressively using the French words *fais do-do* in a song.

Students will accompany a song on a metallophone or glockenspiel, using a simple bordun and shifting triads.

Students will play a B–A–G melody accurately on the recorder.

Students will improvise/compose instrumental accompaniment to a story.

Materials

Music and Instruments

A recording of the song "Bonjour Mes Amis," found on the *Roots and Branches* companion CD; other sources include J. Downing (1998), *From the Gumbo Pot: Stirring Up Tasty Tunes*, and S. Pirtle (2003), *Heart of the World*

Papillion (1998). *Cajun for Kids* CD

The Cajun song "Fais Do-do"

Soprano recorder, glockenspiel, alto metallophone, bass metallophone

Various nonpitched percussion instruments, including instruments commonly found in Cajun music (triangle, washboard, spoons)

Other Resources

Campbell, P. S., E. McCullough-Brabson, and J. C. Tucker. (1994). *Roots and Branches: A Legacy of Multicultural Music for Children* (for reference)

Fleming, C. (2004). *Gator Gumbo: A Spicy-Hot Tale*

Internet sites for dance instructions: www.tabasco.com/music_stage/dance_lessons/index.cfm and www.youtube.com

Map of the United States with New York and Louisiana colored in and connected by a line; a good source for outline maps is Mapquest.com's (2000) *Ready-to-Go Super Book of Outline Maps*

Process

Part I-a

1. Teacher greets students singing verse 1 of the song "Bonjour Mes Amis" (figure 3.1) while shaking hands, greeting, and waving hello to each child.
2. Teacher asks students what the word *bonjour* means, and explains that it is a greeting in French that means "good day," or "hello."
3. Teacher asks students where in the United States they might find people speaking French.
4. Teacher shows students a map of the United States, and asks individuals to trace the route from New York to Louisiana with their fingers.
5. Teacher introduces the term *Cajun* as referring to Americans who live in southern Louisiana and speak French as well as English.
6. Teacher introduces other French words found in the song "Bonjour Mes Amis"; students echo-speak the words while teacher writes the words on the board.
7. Teacher asks students to describe ways people greet each other, either by what they say, or what they do (handshake, high-five, etc.).

Bonjour, Mes Amis

Cajun Folk Song

FIGURE 3.1.   "Bonjour Mes Amis"

8. Teacher sings and/or plays a recording of "Bonjour Mes Amis" and asks students to greet each other during the song using the actions they just discussed.

9. At the conclusion of the song, teacher writes the following words on the board, asking students if they know what any of them mean: *bayou, gumbo, fais do-do.*

10. Teacher defines *bayou* as a swampy, marshy area where Cajun people live; *gumbo* as a thick soup with vegetables, meat, and/or seafood that Cajun people eat; *fais do-do* as a Cajun party where there is lots of singing and dancing to instrument playing.

11. If teacher has access to the CD *Cajun for Kids*, he or she may choose to tell students that they are going to meet a real Cajun person named Papillion, and they should listen carefully to see what they can learn about where Cajuns live, what animals live near them, what they eat, and what they do.

12. Teacher plays track 2 (narration) and then track 1 from the CD (play track 1 through verse 1 only, and fade out).

13. Students answer the questions posed in class discussion.

14. Students and/or teacher identify gumbo as something Cajuns eat, and bayou as a place where they live, writing the words on the board.

15. Teacher asks students if they heard the words *fais do-do* in the song. He or she describes the *fais do-do* as a Cajun party, where there would be lots of singing and dancing to instruments playing.

Part I-b

1. Teacher instructs students in a simple "two-step" dance, first individually, and then with a partner (arms linked). Instructions for dancing the Cajun two-step can be found in the book *Roots and Branches*, or on the websites listed under "Materials."

2. Teacher and students dance the two-step to a recording of any authentic Cajun music, in duple meter. Track 1 from the CD *Cajun for Kids*, "Down on the Bayou," works well.

3. As students sit down, teacher asks students to describe and/or name the instruments they heard. Teacher leads discussion about the instruments found in Cajun music, including but not limited to the instruments heard on the recording used above. It is useful to have actual instruments or pictures of the instruments as visual aids. Some traditional Cajun instruments include the violin (fiddle), accordion, triangle (ti-fer), wooden spoons, and washboard (rubboard).

4. If teacher has access to the CD *Cajun for Kids*, he or she may choose to play sound clips from track 26 (violin, accordion, triangle, washboard, spoons). Actual instruments or pictures of instruments may be used as visual aids.

Part II

1. Teacher explains that the Cajun people love to sing and dance and make music together. Even though a *fais do-do* is a big dance party, it really means "go night-night." It is a lullaby mothers used to sing to their babies, hoping they would fall asleep soon so the mothers could join the party!

2. Teacher sings the song "Fais Do-do" (figure 3.2), in English or French, asking students to count how many times they hear the phrase *fais do-do* (four times).

3. Teacher sings song again, asking students to sing the phrase *fais do-do* each time it happens in the song.

4. Teacher asks students to patsch beat, and to count how many "pats" happen during the A section (eight times). The teacher transfers patschen to bass metallophone (BM).

5. Students take turns playing the BM bordun (see score in figure 3.2).

6. Teacher patsches the alto metallophone (AM) part, asking students to mirror.

7. Teacher sings B section and asks students to count how many times the *pattern* happens (four times).

8. Teacher transfers to AM; students take turns playing.

9. Students sing the A section, and snap on beat 1 of each measure.

10. Teacher asks students to snap, and count how many times it happens (four times).

11. Teacher transfers this to the glockenspiel; students take turns playing.

12. Teacher identifies the song form as ABA, reviewing which instruments play during each section.

13. Students play the ensemble parts while teacher sings.

14. Teacher plays A section on the recorder, asking students what they notice.

15. Students identify the piece as "Fais Do-do," and also identify the pitches used as being B–A–G.

16. Teacher draws pitch stack on the board and points to notes as students play, or teacher asks students to figure out how to play the A section by ear.

17. Some students play A section on recorder, while some accompany on Orff instruments and others may sing the song, as they will have heard it repeatedly by now. Older students may learn to play the entire melody, which uses B, A, G, C^1, and D^1.

Fais Do Do

Cajun Folk Song

Arr. D. Cunningham

FIGURE 3.2. "Fais Do-do"

Part III

1. Teacher explains that Cajun people like to tell stories about living near the bayou. Teacher reviews the definition of a bayou. Teacher asks students to brainstorm what animals live in the bayou, and to listen for the animals in the story.

2. Teacher reads the story *Gator Gumbo* out loud.

3. At the completion of the story, teacher asks students to identify the gumbo ingredients, and lists them on the board (water, crawdads, okra, spices, rice, and the animals).

4. Teacher selects individuals or small groups to represent each ingredient. They must choose a nonpitched percussion instrument to represent them, and create a pattern to play on that instrument. Teacher allows students time to do this.

5. Teacher is the alligator, stirring the gumbo. As teacher points to each student, they jump into the pot (could be a hula hoop) and play their instrument with the pattern they composed. In other words the teacher is the conductor, controlling who jumps in and when they jump in and play. Later, students could be the alligator conductor. Teacher can decide to taste the gumbo, and remove ingredients she or he doesn't want, or add more. Students must play their instruments when they are in the pot. This should sound like layers of ostinati—on other days, teacher may ask students to consider what a simmering pot sounds like, and so forth. This is a good beginning to improvisation, composition, and developing an awareness of what sounds "good"—in other words, artistic discrimination.

6. While collecting the instruments, teacher asks students if they know how to say "good-bye" in French. Teacher says *au revoir*, asking students to echo.

7. Teacher sings "Au Revoir Mes Amis" and waves good-bye to the students. Students also wave good-bye to each other.

Informal Assessment Questions: Cajun Culture

On their way out the door, each student must correctly answer one of the following questions posed by the teacher. If a student does not answer correctly, he/she goes to the back of the line.

Where do Cajun people live?

What language do Cajun people speak?

What is the name of one food that Cajun people like to eat?

What is a *fais do-do*?

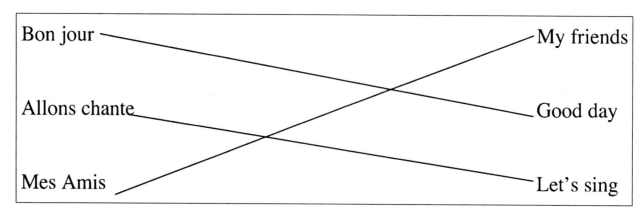

FIGURE 3.3. Matching French to English

What does *bonjour* mean?

What is one instrument you might hear in Cajun music?

Formal Assessment (Written/Oral): Cajun Culture

Students locate (color) Louisiana on a U.S. map, indicating where Cajun people live.

Students write down at least three facts about Cajun culture.

Students sing the song "Bonjour Mes Amis" a capella, in French (as a class).

Students demonstrate knowledge of French phrases by matching them to similar English phrases (see figure 3.3).

Extensions
Other songs, recordings, and literature that pertain to this lesson include "Saute, Crapaud!" from *Roots and Branches*. The book *Petite Rouge* by Mike Artell (2003) is a Cajun version of Little Red Riding Hood—the wolf is an alligator! The illustrations by Jim Harris are excellent, and the text is written in Cajun dialect. A recording of "Le Hoogie Boogie" (The Hokey Pokey) can be found on *Le Hoogie Boogie: Louisiana French Music for Children* by Michael Doucet (1992).

Extensions/Modifications for the Non-Music Educator
Most of this lesson can be taught without having a formal music background. With the exception of the instrumental accompaniment to "Fais Do-do," everything can be done using recordings. Even the song "Fais Do-do" can be found on various commercial recordings available at local bookstores or on the Internet. Many alternate versions of the song exist as well, two of which can be found on the recordings used for this lesson.

There are many ways non-music educators can use this lesson to teach extramusical concepts. French language teachers can explore the French phrases used in the song "Bonjour Mes Amis." As students study Cajun culture, they could develop a schoolwide *fais do-do*, or a parent-student *fais do-do*. Social studies educators could use parts of this lesson to examine the history of how the Cajuns arrived in Louisiana, and compare their experience to that of other ethnic groups residing in North America. English language arts instructors can use the Cajun folktales mentioned in this lesson to examine how this type of literature represents a culture, comparing it to folktales of other cultures. If classroom instruments aren't available, those wanting to engage students in creating their own "gumbo" could have students build and name their own original instruments using everyday materials, creating their own gumbo ingredients.

SLAVERY IN THE NEW WORLD: BRAZIL AND THE UNITED STATES

National Standards

Music

Standard 1: Singing, alone and with others, a varied repertoire of music

Standard 6: Listening to, analyzing, and describing music

Standard 8: Understanding relationships between music, the other arts, and disciplines outside the arts

Standard 9: Understanding music in relation to history and culture

In collaboration with a social studies teacher or alone it is possible to address social studies standards, for example, New York State Social Studies Standards 1, 2, and 3, available at www.emsc.nysed.gov/ciai/standards.html.

The lesson may also address NCTE/IRA English Language Arts Standards 1, 2, and 3, available from www.ncte.org/standards.

Objectives

Students will understand what slavery means to Americans and Brazilians and the societal, moral, and ethical problems that arose from human slavery.

Students will learn about the Underground Railroad through literature.

Students will discuss the situations of risk taking for the slaves and their protectors presented in the video *The Freedom Station*.

Students will understand the importance of dance to contemporary African Americans through Alvin Ailey's choreography for *Revelations*.

Students will understand ways in which slavery in Brazil and in the United States were similar and different.

Students will learn the importance of African music and drumming to Brazilian music tradition through the video, *Olodum: 25 Anos*.

Students will learn to sing the Brazilian folk melody "Cangoma."

Students will learn drumming patterns to accompany the folk melody.

Students will critically reflect on the cost of freedom.

Materials

Books

Levine, E., and L. Johnson. (1993). . . . *If You Traveled on the Underground Railroad*

McGovern, A. (1965). "*Wanted Dead or Alive*": *The True Story of Harriet Tubman*

Videos and Recordings

Diegues, C. (1984). *Quilombo*

The Freedom Station (1998) or *Roots of Resistance: A Story of the Underground Railroad* (1990)

Olodum. (2005). *Olodum: 25 Anos de Samba Reggae e Cidadania* [Olodum: 25 years of samba, reggae, and citizenship]

Revelations, from the video *Ailey Dances* (1986)

Musical Instruments

Drums (floor toms or Brazilian *surdos*) and shakers

Process

Part I

1. Teacher explains that African slavery was a horrific practice in the New World, more specifically, in the United States and in Brazil. For over three hundred years the inhabitants of Brazil lived within a society that not only accepted but also economically depended on slave labor and trade. The economic developments of the 1870s brought small industries to Brazil and, forced by England, in 1850 the country ended the African slave traffic. Contrary to what happened in the United States, where the end of slavery was marked by drastic events culminating in the Civil War, in Brazil abolition happened in steps. The first step was the law of *Ventre Livre* (Free Womb), which in 1871 established that all offspring of slaves would be born free. In 1885 the law *Saraiva-Cotegipe*, known as *Lei dos Sexagenários* (sexagenarian's law) freed all slaves who were sixty-five years of age and older. Finally, on May 13, 1888, the *Lei Áurea* (Aurea Law), signed by Princess Isabel, abolished slavery in Brazil.

2. Teacher introduces the various texts about the Underground Railroad, then divides students into four smaller groups. Each group will read one of the texts. A discussion about the books follows and students share their views.

3. Teacher presents the video *The Freedom Station* or any other visual media that would help students' understanding of the complex relationships of the people involved in the Underground Railroad. For instance, students might think about the risks faced by those who helped the slaves, by those who believed slavery was wrong, or by the slaves who ran away. Teacher shows a map of the Underground Railroad, available at www.nationalgeographic.com/railroad/j1.html or www.pbs.org/wgbh/aia/part4/4p2944.html.

Part II

1. Teacher discusses with students the influence of African music on African American and Brazilian cultures, focusing on the call-and-response form, drumming accompaniment, complex rhythmic layers, and types of instruments.

2. While the initial African music heritage in the United States was vocal, in Brazil this tradition was perpetuated through drumming. The drums became a strong element in Brazilian folk, popular, and classical music. Most of the percussion instruments played nowadays in Brazil are direct descendants of the ones brought from Africa. Among the Brazilian percussion instruments are the *surdo, timbau, ganzá, alfaia* (figure 3.4), *agogô* (figure 3.5), *repenique* (figure 3.6), and *zambumba*.

3. Teacher presents the slavery resistance movement in the *quilombos*, showing parts of the Brazilian movie *Quilombo*.

    Quilombos [ki 'lõ bos] were safe havens for runaway slaves in the northeastern region of Brazil. It is estimated that between eleven thousand and thirty thousand people found refuge in the *quilombos*. The word *quilombo*, which means "military village," comes from the language *Quimbundo*, a Bantu language spoken by Angolans in Africa. *Quilombola* [ki lõ 'bɔ la] designates an inhabitant of the *quilombo*.

FIGURE 3.4.   Pen and Ink *Alfaia* by Annie Detrick © 2009. Used with permission

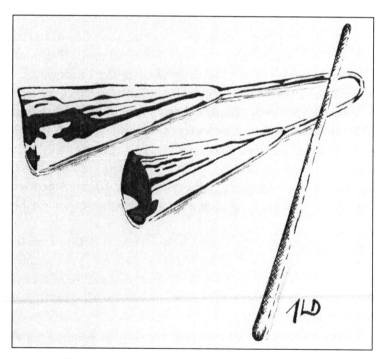

FIGURE 3.5.   Pen and Ink *Agogô* by Annie Detrick © 2009. Used with permission

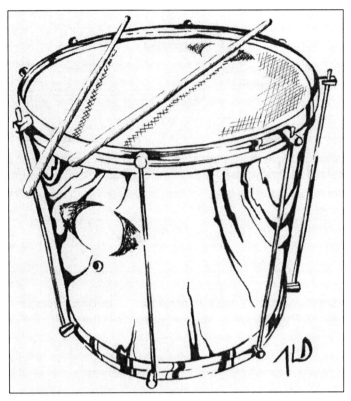

FIGURE 3.6.   Pen and Ink *Repenique* by Annie Detrick © 2009. Used with permission

In the *quilombos* the land belonged to everyone; each person was responsible for cultivating a small part of the land. The *quilombolas* tried to live the life they had lived in Africa by re-creating their African culture. They kept their religious beliefs, eating habits, rituals, community gatherings, music, and dance.

The most well-known *quilombo* to this day is *Quilombo dos Palmares*, whose leader was Zumbi. *Quilombo dos Palmares* lasted for nearly one hundred years and was located in the state of Pernambuco in the northeast region of Brazil. The slaves who lived in this particular refuge were armed and prepared to defend the place with violent military strategies. There were several unsuccessful attempts to destroy and conquer this *quilombo* until finally it succumbed to the Portuguese Crown during the period 1694–1695. Zumbi dos Palmares escaped the attacks, but was ultimately killed in an ambush on November 20, 1695. In honor of Zumbi dos Palmares, an icon of slavery resistance, November 20 is the National Day of Black Awareness in Brazil.

4. Students compare and contrast the events of the Underground Railroad and the *quilombos*, discussing what they accomplished as resistance movements, using the Underground Railroad and *quilombos* worksheet.

5. Students sing the song "Cangoma" (figure 3.7) and play the samba rhythms (figure 3.8) on the drums. It is important to note that the word *ngoma* means "drum" in the Bantu language.

Portuguese: *Tava durumindo, Cangoma me chamou*

IPA: *['tava duɾu'mĩndu kã'goma mi ʃa'mow]*

Translation: *I was sleeping and Cangoma called me*

Portuguese: *Disse: "Levanta, povo, cativeiro já acabou."*

FIGURE 3.7.   "Cangoma"

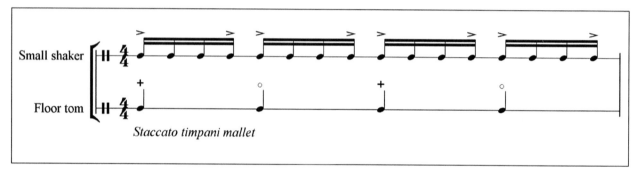

FIGURE 3.8.   Samba Rhythm

IPA: *[di'si le'vāta 'povu katʃi'vejɾu ʒa aka'bow]*

Translation: *It told me: "Get up, people, slavery is over."*

Part III

1. Students watch *Revelations,* choreographed and performed by the Alvin Ailey Dance Company. Students iden-tify the African American elements in the video (the African American spirituals, certain movements that can be traced to West African dance, and social and cultural elements such as the African American church setting in the American South).
2. Students watch a short video of the Brazilian musical group, Olodum, and discuss the African elements present in the music (the layering of rhythms, the drums, and so on).

Learning Outcomes

Students demonstrate understanding of the Underground Railroad through verbalization of important points presented in the video *The Freedom Station* and in the websites.

Students compare and contrast slavery resistance and the search for freedom in the Underground Railroad and the *quilombos* (worksheet).

Students discuss as a class and verbalize important aspects of African American music and its relevance to American and Brazilian music today.

Students perform the song "Cangoma" in Portuguese, accompanied by the drums.

Students demonstrate their understanding of the issues regarding slavery in Brazil and in the United States by writing an essay titled "The Cost of Freedom." The essay should be two to three pages long. Accuracy of information as well as writing accuracy will be assessed.

Underground Railroad and *Quilombos* Worksheet		
	Underground Railroad	*Quilombos*
What happened?		
Who participated?		
Why did it happen?		
When did it happen?		
Where did it happen?		

Additional Resources

Winter, J. (1988). *Follow the Drinking Gourd.*

Hopkinson, D. (1993). *Sweet Clara and the Freedom Quilt.*

Vaughn, M., and L. Johnson. (2001). *The Secret to Freedom.*

CELEBRATING SPIRITUALS

National Standards

Music

Standard 1: Singing, alone and with others, a varied repertoire of music

Standard 2: Performing on instruments, alone and with others, a varied repertoire of music

Standard 9: Understanding music in relation to history and culture

If working alone or in collaboration with the language arts teacher, address the NCTE/IRA English Language Arts Standards 3, 4, and 11, available at www.ncte.org/standards.

It is possible to also address National Social Studies Geography Standard 4 and U.S. History Standards 3 and 4, available at www.educationworld.com/standards/national/soc_sci/index.shtml.

Objectives

Students will identify the textual and musical characteristics found in spirituals.

Students will examine the spiritual song and its place in African American culture through exposure to music and literature.

Students will sing, accurately and on pitch, well-known spirituals.

Students will aurally identify call-and-response form.

Students will accurately perform melodic and rhythmic accompaniment on pitched and nonpitched percussion, on the recorder, and through movement.

Students will perform in a class ensemble.

Materials

Music and Instruments

One or more recordings of "Wade in the Water"; two fine recordings are on K. Harris and R. Harris (1998), *Steal Away: Songs of the Underground Railroad* and the Staple Singers (1991), *Freedom Highway*

Barred instruments (Orff instrumentarium, if possible)

Nonpitched percussion instruments, including hand drums and conga drums

Soprano recorder

Books and Visual Aids

Winter, J. (1988). *Follow the Drinking Gourd*

Visual with the lyrics to the song "Follow the Drinking Gourd"

Visual with the lyrics to the song "Wade in the Water"

An actual drinking gourd, or regular gourd

Spirituals assessment worksheet

Process

Part I

1. Teacher reads the book *Follow the Drinking Gourd* to the class, but sings the sections that contain the song lyrics.

2. Teacher discusses the meaning of the text by soliciting student ideas. He or she asks students if they know what a drinking gourd is, and why/how it was used. If possible, the teacher brings an actual gourd to class as a visual prop. Teacher draws a picture of the Big and Little Dipper on the board and points out the North Star. Class discusses the symbolism in the text and the history of the Underground Railroad. The inside front cover and preface of the book provide excellent information on this topic.

3. Teacher explains that "Follow the Drinking Gourd" (figure 3.9) is an example of a type of song known as a spiritual. He or she continues by explaining that spirituals have their roots in African culture and were sung during the period of slavery in the United States. Teacher gives examples of spirituals that students might already know, such as "Swing Low, Sweet Chariot," "Get on Board, Little Children," and "Somebody's Knocking at Your Door."

4. Teacher presents the characteristics commonly found in spirituals, including hidden meanings, code words, symbolism, repeated lyrics, expression of feelings, religious references, verse-and-refrain form, and call-and-response form, listing these on the board.

5. Teacher sings all or part of the song "Follow the Drinking Gourd" again, asking students to listen for the characteristics from the list on the board. Teacher facilitates their findings, noting that not all spirituals contain all the characteristics.

6. Teacher sings the song again, asking students to sing the phrase "follow the drinking gourd" when it happens in the song, as well as the refrain.

7. Teacher lists various "code" words on the board that are associated with slavery and the Underground Railroad. Some examples are *agent, conductor, freedom train, passenger, safe house, station,* and *promised land.* Teacher asks students to brainstorm what each term means.

8. Teacher introduces the rhythmic ostinati that provide the accompaniment to the song using text, movement, and body percussion, asking students to explain the symbolism of each. Teacher encourages students to create their own movements to complement the text of each ostinato.

9. Teacher introduces the melodic ostinati by mirroring body percussion, and then transferring to barred instruments. The alto xylophone part may be sung as well as played.

10. Teacher introduces the soprano recorder (SR) part either by rote, using a pitch stack, or by note reading from the board.

11. Teacher and students put the ensemble together, layering in the parts one at a time. Soloists may be chosen to sing the verses or teacher may sing verses and students sing refrain. It is useful to have a visual of the text if student soloists are used. Some students may continue to perform the ostinati using movement rather than instruments.

12. Some students may sing the melody while acting out the song as well. For example, a small group can act out a journey on the Underground Railroad, looking to the sky for guidance, seeking pathways, and moving quietly and carefully.

Note: There is some controversy over whether or not "Follow the Drinking Gourd" is an authentic spiritual. There is much evidence to suggest that it is a composed song that was written after the period of slavery in the United States, and not sung by the slaves at all. For this lesson, its authenticity is not overly important as it provides an evocative introduction to the historical importance of spirituals and the presence and purpose of the Underground Railroad, laying the groundwork for further exploration of this period in American history.

Follow the Drinking Gourd

FIGURE 3.9.   "Follow the Drinking Gourd"

FIGURE 3.9.   "Follow the Drinking Gourd"

Follow the Drinking Gourd Verses 2 – 4:

VERSE 2
The riverbank makes a very good road,
The dead trees will show you the way,
Left foot, peg foot, traveling on,
Follow the drinking gourd.

VERSE 3
The river ends between two hills,
Follow the drinking gourd.
There's another river on the other side,
Follow the drinking gourd.

VERSE 4
When the great big river meets the little river,
Follow the drinking gourd.
For the old man is a-waiting for to carry you to freedom
If you follow the drinking gourd.

Part II

1. Students listen to a recording of "Wade in the Water." Teacher asks students to think about the song's meaning and its musical form.

2. Students identify the song as using call-and-response form, in addition to verse and refrain. Students should also recognize the textual symbolism and identify the song as a spiritual, recalling the list of characteristics created earlier.

3. Teacher and students discuss the symbolism of the lyrics, noting their religious significance, as well as their practical significance for escaping slaves. Teacher recalls the book *Follow the Drinking Gourd*, and reviews how the dogs could not track human scent in the water.

4. Teacher introduces the refrain (chorus) and response from "Wade in the Water" (figure 3.10). Teacher sings call, while students sing response and chorus.

5. Students learn the rhythmic and melodic ostinati using the same process as used in "Follow the Drinking Gourd." Again, students may create their own movements to illustrate the ostinati.

6. Teacher and students put the ensemble together, layering in the parts one at a time. Teacher may choose soloists to sing the call, or may sing the call and ask the students to sing the responses and chorus. Again, a visual of the lyrics may be helpful. Some students may continue to perform the ostinati using movement rather than instruments. Other students may sing the melody while acting out the song as well.

7. During the song refrain, teacher encourages students to move about like they are "wading" in the water. During the verses, these students should freeze in place for visual effect.

Part III

Both pieces may be performed together, using the bass xylophone or bass metallophone (BX/BM) to connect the two. At the conclusion of "Follow the Drinking Gourd," the BX/BM should begin to change to the "go, go, children go" pattern from "Wade in the Water." The other parts can layer in from there. This transition can also be a time for the students who were moving and singing to switch to instruments, while the students who were playing instruments now become singers/movers.

Learning Outcomes

Students sing expressively using appropriate phrasing and intonation, as rehearsed in class.

Students perform as an ensemble and demonstrate the ability to maintain a steady beat using appropriate dynamics and to make smooth transitions between sections.

Students appropriately and creatively respond to music through movement.

Students articulate an understanding of the characteristics of spirituals and their role in American history.

Wade in the Water

FIGURE 3.10.   "Wade in the Water"

Wade in the Water

FIGURE 3.10. "Wade in the Water"

Assessment Tools

Digitally record the classroom performance. Watch it as a class and have each student assess the class using the classroom performance rubric.

Distribute and evaluate the spirituals assessment.

Classroom Performance Assessment Rubric

Directions: Please carefully watch and listen to the digital recording of our class performance, and rate it using each of the following items, with 3 being the highest score possible for each item.

1. We sang "Follow the Drinking Gourd" and/or "Wade in the Water" expressively by using energy and appropriate phrasing, and by singing in tune.

3	2	1

2. In our ensemble we kept the tempo steady.

3	2	1

3. In our instrumental ensemble we used appropriate dynamics so that the singing could be heard.

3	2	1

4. As an ensemble, we made smooth transitions between each section of the performance.

3	2	1

5. Our movements appropriately represented the messages found in each song.

3	2	1

Total: _____/15

Spirituals Assessment

Circle the following characteristics you *might* find in a spiritual:

Verse and refrain	References to animals	Religious references
Secret codes	Call-and-response form	Repeated lyrics
Reference to freedom	French and Spanish lyrics	Directions to the corner store

List two of the spirituals that we have sung in music class this year, and for each one, list two characteristics that make it a spiritual.

1. Name of spiritual:

Two characteristics:

2. Name of spiritual:

Two characteristics:

Write a brief paragraph stating who originally sang spirituals, and why.

References

BOOKS AND ARTICLES

Adler, D. A., and S. Byrd. (1992). *A Picture Book of Harriet Tubman*. New York: Holiday House.

Anderson, W. M., and P. S. Campbell. (1996). *Multicultural Perspectives in Music Education* (second ed.). Reston, VA: MENC.

Anderson, W. M., and M. Moore. (1998). *Making Connections: Multicultural Music and the National Standards*. Reston, VA: MENC.

Andrews, L. J., and P. E. Sink. (2002). *Integrating Music and Reading Instruction: Teaching Strategies for Upper-Elementary Grades*. Reston, VA: MENC.

Anti-Defamation League, USC Shoah Foundation Institute, and Yad Vashem. (2005). *Echoes and Reflections: A Multimedia Curriculum on the Holocaust*. New York: Author.

Artell, M. (2003). *Petite Rouge*. New York: Puffin.

Barrett, J. R., C. W. McCoy, and K. K. Veblen. (1997). *Sound Ways of Knowing: Music and the Interdisciplinary Curriculum*. New York: Schirmer Books.

Brian, A. (1999). *The Night Has Ears: African Proverbs*. New York: Atheneum.

Buckley, R. (2002). *The Wing*. Nashville, TN: Abingdon Press.

Burton, B. (1993). *Moving within the Circle: Contemporary Native American Music and Dance*. Danbury, CT: World Music Press.

Campbell, P. S. (2004). *Teaching Music Globally: Experiencing Music, Expressing Culture*. New York: Oxford University Press.

Campbell, P. S., E. McCullough-Brabson, and J. C. Tucker. (1994). *Roots and Branches: A Legacy of Multicultural Music for Children*. Danbury, CT: World Music Press.

Cassino, M., and J. Nelson. (2009). *The Story of Snow: The Science of Winter's Wonder*. San Francisco: Chronicle Books.

Choksy, L., and D. Brummit. (1987). *120 Singing Games and Dances for Elementary Schools*. Englewood Cliffs, NJ: Prentice Hall.

Consortium of National Arts Education Associations. (1994). *National Standards for Arts Education: What Every Young American Should Know and Be Able to Do in the Arts*. Reston, VA: MENC.

Corona, L. (2000). *Brazil: Modern Nations of the World*. San Diego, CA: Lucent Books.

Crook, L. (2009). *Music of Northeast Brazil* (second ed.). New York: Routledge.

Enciclopédia de Música Brasileira: Popular, Erudita, e Folclórica [Encyclopedia of Brazilian music: Popular, classic, and folk]. (1998). São Paulo: Publifolha.

Fausto, B. (2008). *A Concise History of Brazil* (twelfth ed.). New York: Cambridge University Press.

Fleming, C. (2004). *Gator Gumbo: A Spicy-Hot Tale.* New York: Melanie Kroupa Books.

Hopkinson, D. (1995). *Sweet Clara and the Freedom Quilt.* New York: Dragonfly Books.

Kain, C. J. (1997). American Humanities Studies: A Multicultural, Interdisciplinary Approach in the English Classroom: Learning Levels 11–14. PhD dissertation, University of Nebraska. *Dissertation Abstracts International, 58-06A,* 2038.

Larson, D. A. (1998). A Study of, and the Effects of, Multicultural Understandings through a Multicultural Music Curriculum, Specifically in Two Predominantly European American Communities of Southwest Minnesota. Master's thesis, Southwest State University. *Master's Abstracts International,* 38-05, 1154.

Lattuca, L. R., L. J. Voigt, and K. Q. Fath. (2004). Does Interdisciplinarity Promote Learning? Theoretical Support and Researchable Questions. *Review of Higher Education 28* (1), 23–48.

Levine, E., and L. Johnson. (1993). *. . . . If You Traveled on the Underground Railroad.* New York: Scholastic.

Levine, E., and K. Nelson. (2007). *Henry's Freedom Box: A True Story from the Underground Railroad.* New York: Scholastic.

Levine, R. (2003). *The History of Brazil.* New York: Palgrave McMillan.

Libbrecht, K. (2003). *The Snowflake: Winter's Secret Beauty.* Stillwater, MN: Voyageur Press.

Mapquest.com. (2000). *Ready-to-Go Super Book of Outline Maps.* New York: Scholastic.

Martin, J. B. (1998). *Snowflake Bentley.* New York: Houghton Mifflin.

Martinez, M., and E. Roscetti. (2003). *World Beat Rhythms beyond the Drum Circle: Brazil.* Milwaukee, WI: Hal Leonard.

Mathieson, C. F. (1996). *Music of Many Cultures.* Greensboro, NC: Mark Twain Media/Carson Dellosa Publishing Company.

McGovern, A. (1965). *"Wanted Dead or Alive": The True Story of Harriet Tubman.* New York: Scholastic.

Nketia, J. H. K. (1974). *The Music of Africa.* New York: W.W. Norton & Company.

Oceana Books. (2007). *Butterflies: A Fascinating Guide to This Beautiful Insect Species.* London: Quantum Publishing.

Polacco, P. (2000). *The Butterfly.* New York: Philomel Books.

Quesada, R. (1998). *When the Road Is Long, Even Slippers Feel Tight: A Collection of Latin American Proverbs.* Riverside, NJ: Andrews McMeel.

Sabanovich, D. (2004). *Brazilian Percussion Manual: Rhythms and Techniques with Application for the Drum Set.* Van Nuys, CA: Alfred Publishing.

Salerno, S. (2006). *Viagem pelo Brasil em 52 histórias* [Traveling around Brazil in 52 stories]. São Paulo: Companhia das Letrinhas.

Shinnar, L. (2006). *The Butterfly and the Flame and Other Stories of Jewish Life from Krakow to Israel.* Jerusalem: Mazo Publishers.

Skidmore, T. E. (2010). *Brazil: Five Centuries of Change* (second ed.). New York: Oxford University Press.

Stern, A. (1996). *Tales from Many Lands: An Anthology of Multicultural Folk Literature.* Lincolnwood, IL: National Textbook Company.

Titon, J. T. (Ed.). (2009). *Worlds of Music: An Introduction to the Music of the World's People* (third ed.). Belmont, CA: Schirmer Cengage Learning.

Vaughan, M., and L. Johnson. (2001). *The Secret to Freedom*. New York: Lee & Low Books.

Volavková, H. (Ed.) (1993). *. . . I Never Saw Another Butterfly . . .: Children's Drawings and Poems from Terezín Concentration Camp, 1942–1944* (second ed.). New York: Schoken Books.

Wade, B. C. (2004). *Thinking Musically: Experiencing Music, Expressing Culture*. New York: Oxford University Press.

Waldman, N. (2003). *The Snowflake*. Brookfield, CT: Millbrook Press.

Wiggins, J. (2001). *Teaching for Musical Understanding*. New York: McGraw-Hill.

Winter, J. (1988). *Follow the Drinking Gourd*. New York: Dragonfly Books.

Withers-Ross, H. K. (1999). *Multicultural Folksongs in Presenting Cultures in a Sixth-Grade Social Studies Classroom*. Unpublished PhD dissertation, University of South Carolina.

Zona, G. A. (1994). *The Soul Would Have No Rainbow If the Eyes Had No Tears and Other Native American Proverbs*. New York: Touchstone.

SOUND AND VIDEO RECORDINGS

Alvin Ailey American Dance Theater. (1986). *Ailey Dances*. VHS. West Long Branch, NJ: Kultur Video.

Convery, R. (1991). "At Terezín." Sound recording. Corvallis, OR: Earthsongs.

Downing, J. (1998). *From the Gumbo Pot: Stirring Up Tasty Tunes*. CD. New Orleans: Johnette Downing.

Diegues, C. (1984). *Quilombo*. DVD. New Yorker Video.

Doucet, M. (1992). *Le Hoogie Boogie: Louisiana French Music for Children*. CD. Burlington, VT: Rounder Records.

The Freedom Station. (1998). VHS. Charlotte, NC: PBS Home Video.

Harris, K., and R. Harris. (1998). *Steal Away: Songs of the Underground Railroad*. CD. Westchester, PA: Appleseed Recordings.

Olodum. (2005). *Olodum: 25 Anos de Samba Reggae e Cidadania* [Olodum: 25 years of samba, reggae, and citizenship]. DVD. São Paulo: Globo Video.

Papillion. (1998). *Cajun for Kids*. CD. Redway, CA: Music for Little People.

Pirtle, S. (2003). *Heart of the World*. CD. Albany, NY: A Gentle Wind.

Roots of Resistance: A Story of the Underground Railroad. (1990). VHS. Alexandria, VA: PBS Video.

Schafer, R. M. (1992). *Snowforms*, recorded by Elektra Women's Choir, on *Elektra Women's Choir*. CD. Peterborough, Ontario: Skylark Music.

The Staple Singers. (1991). *Freedom Highway*. CD. New York: Legacy.

Tropical Rainforest. (2005). DVD. Sherman Oaks, CA: Slingshot.

Breinigsville, PA USA
20 January 2011
253809BV00002B/1/P

9 781607 093114